Save As

Save As

A. Frances Johnson

PUNCHER & WATTMANN

First published in 2021
Published by Puncher and Wattmann
PO Box 279
Waratah NSW 2298

http://www.puncherandwattmann.com
puncherandwattmann@bigpond.com

NATIONAL LIBRARY OF AUSTRALIA

A catalogue entry for this book is available from the National Library of Australia.

ISBN   9781922571106

Cover design by Miranda Douglas
Typesetting by Morgan Arnett
Printed by Lightning Source International

Cover image © The Field Museum
www.flickr.com/photos/field_museum_library/3349699278
Title: Moon Model
Description: Prepared by Johann Friedrich Julius Schmidt, Germany in 1898.
Made of 116 sections of plaster on a framework of wood and metal.
Field Columbian Museum West Court Alcove 103.
Original size and material: 11x14 inch glass negative
Digital Identifier: CSGEO12536
Part of the Illinois Urban Landscapes Project:
www.fieldmuseum.org/urbanlandscapes

Contents

The flag's taking off for that filthy place, and our jargon's drowning out the drums.
... On to the wasted and dried-up countries! – at the service of the most monstrously
efficient military-industrial complexes.
Goodbye to here, forget what's there.
... Not caring for science, eager for comforts – let the rest of the world go blow!

Arthur Rimbaud, *A Season in Hell*

Nature is a scene by Casper David Friedrich
It points to a place beyond peaks and pinnacles
And seems to redeem the general pillage
But children circle the garbage piles
And subject to cycles the world is volatile
The cycle of violence is a manner of speaking

Evelyn Reilly, 'Broken Water'

For Grace Johnson

Part One: Save Us

Daughter of lead

I was a daughter of lead, petrol my childhood.
Bowser and breast fed the same rush —
stains on the drive sump lakes for doll picnics.
'Nice clean Amoco' was seatbeltless.
The futura was Ford. OPEC. Crude.
Combustible plant and animal corpses.
Now I lie down with them, asserted
by my dad's tarnished Caltex tie pin.

I was a daughter of lead, petrol a soundtrack
of bowsered base, concerts I could not go to,
a filtered perfume inhaled like any drug.
My mother drove the 'old bomb' I later drove
to casual jobs; fan-belted pantyhose and broken
radio signs of lives stalled. I drove late.
My first car, a rusted column-shift, cost
nine-hundred waitressing dollars. I paid a man
to haul it to landfill, bury it above the seam.

I was a daughter of lead, car warmer than
my rented room. I idled outside, heater on high.
Vegetable fuels date from the 1950s, my smart
girlfriend said. I craved poetry dating, not carbon.
She insisted I meet her brother, testing plant-based
fuels in her family's Fawkner garage.
There was no will to market zese fuels, Horst said,
all romantic. We never went for a drive.

I am still that daughter — petrol my stinking rag,
litred clock and borrowed bone-shop. I burn it

as I tree-plant over rhythmic frack and fear.
The oxymoron is me, guzzling at the teat
as wildfire jumps the freeway — as if the way
were ever free. Smoke insinuates through
the vents of my fourth car, nervy fuel
gauge demanding veined hits.
I do not leave the vehicle. I do not leave it.
I cannot drive the crude world home.

My father's thesaurus

You drove faultlessly until sundown.
As dusk fell, trees lit Magritte black,
discreet ideas of near and far
merged, and your words, *sotto voce*
then *forte*, rolled out, a new Babel
of half-familiar phrases, expletives,
vigilant accountancies, cornball song,
plant catalogues and chess moves.

That the banks could not be trusted
was a saying you'd taken for granted
since the Great Depression. Now the
phrase bloomed in your brain. At dinner
you said, for reasons of efficiency:
the banks were past the mustard.
We lovingly accepted the joke, while
in the wet yard the dog chased its tail,
saw nothing loveless to incriminate.

Later, fear grew: school-tie gerontologists,
nurses, phone calls, bills – lacking tact.
Sheet music's random dots perplexed,
rainspots bearing no relation to the cruel
beauty of pianos. All could betray,
induce the agitation of sunsets.
You watched the piano and played
the sunset. You insisted: every good boy
deserved flight, all cows ate gravel.

We read your blended agendas uneasily,
concealing our weakness at multiple choice.

All too soon, random hatred arrived with
show-girl fanfare, disfiguring your old kindness.
For peace, we concurred on a mattress bank;
the district nurse *was* trying to poison you.
Most days, words aligned, neat as jam jars,
the fruity, sunny order of Fowlers Vacola,
your late mother's preserves.

We played codebreakers as evening fell,
winning small semantic wars, fighting
through thickets of translation,
gardening gloveless in your wildering
flowerbeds. One night you drove the car
into the garage wall, blue shoe on
the accelerator, brown on the brake.
With a bang, words collided around
your head like trams not yet waited for.
The foul sunset was to blame. A week later

suspension came, plotted by a gimlet-eyed
medico. We failed the first test with you,
then the second, weeping in the Colac Coles
carpark, lost trolleys whirring and clacking.
You'd driven at snail pace on country roads
then rocketed across a petunia'd town
roundabout, a bollard bent beneath
the wheel. *This betrayal,* you said, having
never brooked a fine, *was the bitter end.*
The nuances of fast and slow, slow then fast,
cannot be understood by criminals. We hung
our heads and hid the report in the glovebox,
not accepting a dickey wheel.

My mother and I drove you home from the test
among paddocks and cattle, vast distances
suddenly too close, like a bellicose
stranger with foul breath, strained sun
falling like a thief behind the hill.
It, too, had been a shamer, a radiant form
with a signature. None of us spoke or
decoded. There was nothing left but to hack
through the last forests until the axe
quietened, and you were half-calm
in night's velvety armchair, dog roiling
at your feet like a spinning top.
I had one just like it once, you confided
after furious silence and tea, taking my hand,
turning it round and round, bemused,
as if you wanted to test it, detach it and send it
whirring into the cold, free universe.

Threshold

At the front door, my best uncle
offers lemonade to snow-collared
Seven-Day Adventists. It's 45 degrees
at the neck, at the foot of the cross.
He has his own faith, he says, cool pastures,
a shepherd to guide him, but thank you,
all the best. Later, he scratches his head.
The paddock is fried, the earth that
the meek will inherit compacted.
Nowhere's cool. The kitchen clock rivets
time as flies of keen intellect study
the cream sill. Most days, his late wife
hovers, makes cheerful lists by
detonating whitegoods. On TV,
a sagging pollie bursts into view,
a red-eyed, akubra'd succubus.
Nation's smoking vale.
Thou art with me and thy rod,
he sighs, turning it off and upping
the air con. But rod, white noise and fly
conspire, arhythmic; Glad-wrapped
steak and veg sweat sanguine economies.
Next day, lodged in his plump recliner,
the knocking starts again. His topped-up
glass falls; his pencilled raceguide
floats down, takes third place
after his body. He won't answer,
but still outsmarts the wily sun,
knocking and rapping, wanting
to slake its thirst, needing a tip

on the fourth at Randwick,
to be lead to quiet waters by.

Ring-in

For Roma Johnson (1932–2017) and Jane Woollard

I collect your wedding rings in a rainy satellite town of failing industry;
rats disguised as seagulls hurl above antennas, distant spires, Maccas'
    roofline.
My friend drives, lamb-like behind the wheel, gentle with speed limits,
a processional reprise. We find the place, a plain Besser-brick parlour
framed in doric grief, the short drive massed with orphaned
icebergs that can never know life as a true rose.

The boy—angel with cornrows and bad tie has kept the 'shop' open
a notch past five. We are late for the rings and he is 'outa here!'
for 'fish-and-chip Friday'. When he smiles wide, I see his fillings
are as old as mine, dark insets like small coals or a mouthful of flies.
The angel hands me a paper bag. I expect 'Safeway' printed on one side,
reeling back at the assault of trace sweat and Cacharel (those tiring
missions to find you old stock), the slam of lanolin-greased memory.

I can't hear against the rain's dolorous half-rhyme, and you, you are typing
on the roof, on your old Scalextric, drawing breath, corrector ribbon
running out and out. *Tsk, tsk, tsk.* But my friend, not rain, is tapping at
    the glass,
is flowers contained in all seasons, brolly holding sky. The vast bag contains
a tiny faux-suede pouch, company logo in flocked gold. And two rings
to round me out (your sparkle-hand again), milk-eyed diamonds,
midget sapphire, daggy stainless band all dad could afford.

We drive off together, all three, your sun-spotted ghost-hand in mine,
rings tight, but not tight enough; this unbearable ring, a ringing in,
I peer through the wet windscreen, wiper blades noisy, ragged gulls
    arguing

for chips and a decent bird book entry. I see my friend is crying.
But me, I am desperate to spot a true rose.

Bypass town

The town café never took off; stale
lamingtons and weak cappuccino served
by a mortgagee farmer, unskilled at
roasting, price hikes, false charm.

I drive to commune with your tea-stained
ghost. Each time I think I'll never
come back. The cairn-like bowser,
dead spider in the lounge cornice,
ironed doilies dissembling.

I drive on empty through ruined
pebble-mix, bird-bath streets,
Tidy Town signs singing rust duets.
On the outskirts, tractor sheds ring
pine plantation gloom, the sick green
shadow to be lopped and cleared.

Inside the dark canopy, I confuse
radio white noise with memory.
I've been here before, am too late.
My sibling has rifled through, hunger
for markers a wombing cry.
I phone my solicitor. *You'll never win*,
she says. *He thrives on going head-to-head.*
Sell it: ride-on, land, furniture, walls.

Next time I visit, the café's boarded up —
grim radiata cropped, bald hills
a sunny alopecia. A lone cow grazes,

unfenced flanks inviting roadkill.
Like us, hills are stumped
by buzz-saws we can't see.

Driving through *pinus radiata*, radio
signals die. A crepe-papered box sits
unsmiling on vinyl. Love, I have come back
for a blue wren teapot, six crocheted
antimacassars, a daphne planter
and the ventricular rictus of a death
certificate, a paper chest.

72 Derwents

I never had 72 Derwents
I had 12, unlike Dolores O'Dea,
the pampered builder's daughter,
thick as a plank and pretty as.
I coveted her acid greens that said
both Lake District and glam rock,
wild persimmons for urgent,
upscaled bubble headings that
reduced the size of an essay.
Her big-drinking dad had no need
of colour or seatbelts, had built half
a cream brick suburb with metal
roller blinds for *I-talian* immigrants.
Success! Everyday a birthday for Dolores,
who donned adult clothes early.
When her dad drove too fast
and too drunk down the Foot Street
rollercoaster and hit a pole, I made
Dolores a card with my Derwents,
thinking two colours tactful, kind.
After the funeral, she wore new
platform shoes to school, which,
at $36.99, were higher and dearer
than any corks I'd ever seen,
a double-strapped, wobbling riot
of green and persimmon.

Succour

Craving sugar, milk and eternal love,
I drew Our Lady of the Perpetual Succour
as crayoned lollipop with massive Buddha
teats. Suckered by the word I later came
to know as 'care', I became a follower
lacking confidence to invent her own
religion. Mary's tiny statue glowed
in a dark I was afraid of.

We bent our heads at mass like small,
wigged robots, admonished to bow
low on the prayer word 'Jesus'.
Je-sus, I chanted carefully, nodding
like a fairground shy, gifted five cents
from my mother's worn fawn purse.
Hot kid palms turned the silver coin over
'til it stank of ore or awe, or a foul thing
fallen from a tooth. My father cuffed me
when I failed to donate to the collection.
I stared down the plate's priestly glare,
its felt mouth, a faded billiard green,
short-changed by junior Judas hands
with an instinct for fee for service.

When I grew and forgot Sunday jobs of bob
and coin my mother's cool, ringed fingers
still glanced my neck, a kind of half-strangle
marking genealogies of bobbing. Dear Jesus,
I became forgetful, hormonal; should I bob
on 'womb' or proper name? I learnt

in science that I too had a womb, though
immaculate conception was held apart.
I hedged my bets, looking for miracles
in a nodding zone between labouring
'woman' and genius 'saviour', sure I'd
be given a treat for inclusive ingenuity.
Instead, I was thought slow, was not
granted pleasure. I did not save.

Later I traded the Latin beauty of *succursus*
(*trans: to run and give help to, succour*)
for wordy enchantments like 'sussurus',
bobbing and bending to a new lord:
poetry and its selfish martyrs. Careless
consonance was mine, vowels as assonant
as too much jam. Now, on a Sunday, I attend
a secular mass of words, sift and sort
half-prayers, ghost-hand pressing my neck.
I bob and nod, drop, breathe and bend.
Neither silver coin nor miracle present,
but now and then small statues of the mind
come to light the blue-robed dark.

Encyclopedia[*]

The gilded A–Z has had its boot
in my neck since '76. Turquoise
and maroon leatherette was a neat
shoe-shop trick, styling empire's
need to know, not understand.

The A–Z favoured talk of elephants (E),
natives (N), copper (C) and nickel (N),
grainy travelogues. Upgrades meant
kaleidoscopic inserts of rare butterflies,
the parrots of Brazil, baseline rewards
for lumpy, flightless children.

Labour was indentured silver-gelatin
smiles, run-off out of frame. Local customs
(dress, ceremony, weaving, song) came after
captain-of-industry monologues – royal
waves affixed a Commonwealth stamp.

When Funk and Wagnalls knocked,
my mother mistook the Jewish-American
brand for German, closed the flywire
against the talking case. When Britannica
knocked, my mother, aproned and harried –
burning dinner (BD), teething baby (TB),

---

[*] Encyclopedia Britannica went out of print in 2012 after 244 years. The Britannica was conceived as a conservative reaction to Denis Diderot's French *Encyclopédie* (published 1751–66), which was widely viewed as subversive. Ironically, the *Encyclopédie* had begun as a French translation of the popular English encyclopedia, *Cyclopaedia*, published by Ephraim Chambers in 1728.

post-natal depression (PND) – asked
the pushy salesman to sit. We'd make
an A–Z of plans she never had. He got
his foot in the door, collected a cheque
and a warm cordial, our mother twisting
her apron and patting her hair.

'Bloody ideas,' shouted dad that night,
sweat-stained and tie loose.
'CALTEX' was gilded on his case, but he
stacked shelves at night to pay off the set.
The A–Z was surely the business of the world,
we thought, recruited young to extractive talk
that never stopped, words mined and spent,
run-off at the mouth, childlike accounts
of profit and loss, exploration, nation.

Thirty years later, I reach for 'B',
my A–Z Google via Encarta.
Under 'Brazil', after forests,
lost parrots roost, shriek
ghostly facts, 'E' for endtime:
Bauxite! Timber! Nickel! Tin! Gold!

I say 'forests'

I say forests are there
though they are not.
I read the stats and tactfully insist.
I can do no more. I eat my sandwich
between glass and concrete
keeps, a bugless greensward.
My job is not connected.

Some say the forest has a dark lung,
was offered a last cigarette in June.
Naysayers! People *live* in forests, I say.
Think quaint songs, woodsy tales
in peasant contralto, crops sprouting
in rainbow sump. The poet's glade. Air.
For these reasons, forests are there.

I said this to a girl child who reminded me
of myself. I told her that red-cloaked heroines
still take covered baskets to grandma's.
But she was carsick from the long trip
through plantation pine and I had a chainsaw
migraine starting. I lay down on the back
seat and made her drive home.
I had the wolf in me that day.

I do my best – make donations,
hike every kind of virtual wood.
Why is the understorey bone quiet?
'Real' forest, I complain, requires
sensurround, full PayPal pastorale.

I want the biscuit crunch of bracken
and babbling brook, gnawing
insect song and scuttling quoll.
They upgrade my app.

In fake valleys, I muse on metaphor's
rich-seeming truth: I'm 'in the wild'
yet not bitten by insects — swarms are
of the airy past. I carry water, food
and first-aid kit, wear good shoes.
But my holiday reading avers
that forests and riparian systems
have vanished, that 'wilderness'
was always violent gazetted scene —
tent, billy and gun painted over
remnant green. When I return
to the city I never left, I cancel
my subscription, water pale potplants
on the sill. I can do no more.

Wrack boys

We never made the team, spent brooding
years collecting paper-thin nautilus and
bleached dream wrack by ruined piers.
We doled out for casks and almost-first
editions, pieces now too rare, like us, for fact.
In silent black polyester, lovingly torn,
we uttered good boy names behind the dune:
Hughes, Heaney, Whitman, Frost,
hoping light peels of page and earth
would reveal loving touches, songs
of ourselves. Cheated of these, rejected
by art schools, we burned the books
in an old tyre and fled from wetland
to pub. Ale froth covered my mate's
bumfluff, his lip tender and pink,
even as he grew to tall violence.
We asked for the bosomless barmaid's
phone number in quavery unison, hoping
for a kindly screw or shared spliff,
sightings of our bewildered selves
in the mirror of a neat, warm flat.
But amber pot glass refracted us
as the rum discards we were.
She would not loan us her mascara,
no, though limp *Flock o' Seagulls* hair
and eighties style was back.
It was true, what was in us, the black
fears and loneliness; we could not look
poem, girl, boy or creature in the eye.
The dishwasher hissed perfect storms

behind the till to back her up.
I read you! Collectors not keepers!
We called her filthy names and left.
I didn't tell my mate that though books
were finished for us, I'd kept some back
from the flames. I rectified this later,
as he snored angrily over his case
in the vacant servo, neck as bent
as plumber's pipe. Outside, waves
gazumped the pier and wind took me
to the end of the line. The cindering
tyre semaphored shooting flame until
our almost-first editions quietened,
no longer sang of book-burnt skies.

The leader's son

The leader's son is fast asleep when called.
He mimes commoner actions: stand, sit,
wave and lie, showing his best side.
Before the cameras roll, he argues
with his dad about the economic stats
of poetry, words never aired nor free
to air. Upon the podium, potted palms
nod dull acquiescence against the flag.
He has not seen his father since
the race began. Minders loom,
weaponised words a security concern.
Their dress code, like his dad's, favours
suited repetition, primaries slaughtering
red and blue, the tie a callibrated rout
at parent–teacher night. He learnt that
politicians' milk-bottle smiles are never
shy, though orthodontal rectitude
suggests the same Canberra dentist.

At 6am next day, make-up arrives
at the family home, pastes over absence
of fatherly contrition. His dad disappears
in beige clouds, bowl of national
cornflakes masticated under rhythmic
buzz and click. Winter sun shafts through,
value-adding transcendence to a dawn cheer
campaign (Brutus knew such camera angles).
Schooled in classics and larrikinese,
the boy gasps when his dad appears on TV
in his favorite cap (the fucker never asked).

The man of the hour twirls it backwards,
forwards, roundabout as if to indicate
a sure youth vote, plasticated mateship.
After the win, the replay soundtracks
to martial pop; party apparatchiks lead
a bosomy cast in wide simple ties,
good shirts unravelling, and all the fearful
chorus put away on remote islands.
The boy is forced to don a sprig
of artificial wattle for another jaundiced
photoshoot, his family *stumm* behind
the everyman who burns the toast
and backhands the dog except on
photo-shoot Sundays. His mother purrs,
demurs and shies, scratching her first-lady
behind with extender talons, thinks
of shopping hard for the role.
Her son's overbite clamps down. He will
now be every, every son, who sits
and stands and waves and lies.

Tour of eyes

What he saw in '68 was not the same as what he saw in '98.
The second time, his older daughter and son-in-law saw it too,
had travelled with him, coming to it differently, the seeing.

Years on, a different daughter holds him at the rock,
sweat patch in the perfect small of her back
something to fasten on, like a lake in the distance.

What he'd seen with his own eyes, this daughter saw
through his wife's cornflower orbs: an inscribed
righteous rock mocked by humid aftermath.

His perpetual tour means seeing day as night,
random sightlines firing; rivers always run red.
Vision is always jungle-framed.

At fighting school he'd no instruction on how not to see
too much or too little; he went and saw it all again,
night in the middle of day, a false peace.

There, over yonder, they tossed the flaming ones,
the round, blinking stone says, a pat tourist guide.
He weeps for the buried eyes that cannot tour

the pretty tow paths, second daughter's hand
striking his like a match inside the fuselage.

The art: Ultramarine

For Helen Creswell and clients, Joel Nafuma Refugee Centre, Rome

There's always art, they tell you.
You look blank. You have nowhere
to sleep, no Carte d'Identita. They bring
sandwiches, a second-hand mobile,
brushes and pens. The phone, an inedible
silver fish in your hand. Who to call?

We want to spend time with you, if you are willing,
the art therapist says. You shrug and oblige.
You appear to spend time, but time's jammed up,
increments of past and present.
You age faster when you are nowhere,
move with an old man's gait.

You draw a boat shape with a scratchy pen.
Apply excess pigment. Why not?
Ultramarine, the therapist calls it.
That's right, the day of ultra marine.
You loosen blue blobs with water.
Soon the whole page is blue, lines lost,
your boat sunk, a whiff of petrol
in your nostrils. Everything ultra ocean.

But the brush, soft and wet, with real hair
relaxes you. You massage blue into paper tooth –
for weeks no other colours interest you.
Then, one day you come back and draw
a horizon line, fill the sky with flowers.
Rosa, jaune, magenta, cerulean, viridian.
The therapist squints at your one-page
world, says, Oh, it's beautiful.

The American embassy holds an exhibition:
OUTSIDER ART. They want you.
They want all fifteen boys from the program.
Seven of you have places to sleep but no work;
three of you now have identity cards;
eight are sleeping rough all up. You have no card,
no work, but you have art and sleep.
Most days you confuse the two.
The colour behind the eye, leaching dark.

They've taken your wreath pictures away
to be framed, the flat blue squares as well.

They go together, you tell the art therapist.
When you get to the exhibition, you aren't let in
by the uniformed man with the gun,
even though you have washed your
clothes at the centre and are looking smart.
You have no identity card, no paper or brush.
The art therapist and the other people
are already inside. You have arrived
foolishly late, but are nowhere still.

Violet, you have learnt from the therapist,
is the color at the end of the visible spectrum
of light between blue and invisible ultraviolet.
The colour of mist and amethyst and not seeing.
Purple twilight infuses exhaust, petrol.
You breathe deep. Heads of commuters bob
around you as if you were already drowned.

You stand a while among expensive cars,
light a cigarette. Then another. An hour later,
after the speeches, the art therapist calls

the silver fish, which makes a thin trumpet sound.
You hear her kind voice say your name.
Art is not helping, you say, and start to cry.
She runs down the grand scala, strappy sandals
typing on marble. She carries a long list;
it flutters behind her like a stole.
She gives you a hug, crushing the print-out
between you. I'm so sorry, she says.

You go inside to see the guard.
I've forgotten my glasses, she says.
But his name – she points vaguely to a place
in the spiraling document – is here.
The guard is silent and does not smile;
you don't smile either, you begin to shake.
You want to shake your pictures
until frame and glass shatter,
take them back to the sea.
His name is here, she insists.
She takes your arm and leads you up
to where your art swells
and subsides, a hung sea.

Her modern

It can happen anytime. The wrong brush,
snowfalls in the wrong hemisphere.
The dawning of misjudgement,
the way it went: his pictures,
completed in days, yours
taking upwards of a year.

You were tumescent with ideas,
they woke you, wanted you.
You worked hard. Sex became
boring. Like poverty.
Still, you kept working.
You'd rather slit your wrists
than teach. You backed yourself.

You were smart enough to know
epoch, like religion, was a sham.
Modernity is a qualitative,
not a chronological, category.
Still, you could have stolen the show,
shown the steal. This you imagined,
fiercely, before trading closed.

The young boy painters
(one of whom you loved –
technique half-arsed) became
overnight *enfant terribles*
ordained by start-up gallerists,
they of the auctionable geometric hair
and bankrolled husbands.

Both confused French theory with power,
gesture with god. Or the devil.

If the stable boys play-acted
avant-garde, unwashed genius,
curatorial reverence compounded.
They never confessed to anything
oedipal. They hadn't wanted
periods, just to be part of one.
Fuck them all, they said, classically.
Fuck art, they added, half-heartedly.

When you said it, it meant something
less and more radical. Your refusal
to capitulate to expectation was sexy.
You didn't do 'wimmins art'.
Back then, no-one conjured art
as an absence of heroics. You were happy
for their success. The boys said
they'd make sure you wouldn't starve.
That's what they said, at the time.

These days you drive yourself
into stone feature walls, tidy up
kiddie art in thin, day-glo acrylic.
Your dreams: carmine, Indian red,
cadmium, umber — pure synaesthesia.
Your marriage: colourless safety.

In the bush garden, over your lucky spade,
a big brown snake rises up. You remember
one dark painting, heavy to lift. A riotous
Eden with poisonous overglaze;

a painting to trouble the world
before you knew what 'world' was.
You lift the spade high, a master
stroke, invite colour back home.

Part Two: Save As

It burns my eyes to turn to hers, my wide brown land out of like hands
but traced in fetish verse—
'I love a sunburnt country'   *I loved a sunburnt country.*
                                                  I loved white nativity
that digs its roots and ticks to suck the floodplains and the sea—
The love that swept those sweeping plains from Nan, from Mum, from me.

Alison Whittaker, 'A Love Like Dorothea's'

Attachment to the One True Place is no guarantee of honour to
other places, and certain modes of attachment may even require the
degradation of other places. The British Royal Family loves Balmoral,
and they see to the protection and improvement of this place, but their
care is made possible by the fact that they have their money invested
in a swag of companies that are despoiling systematically other
people's places, and relations of power embedded in the commodity
ensure that they need neither know nor care about those places.
… The indigenous criterion reveals, as denied or shadow places,
all those places that produce or are affected by the commodities you
consume, places consumers don't know about, don't want to know about,
and in a commodity regime don't ever need to know about or take
responsibility for.

Val Plumwood, 'Shadow places and the politics of dwelling'

The violent trees

Sometimes I yearn to wrestle a young gum
to ground so suddenly it can't react.
But I know its brother-trees and tree cops
would rush me, load me up as if I was dying for it.
From then on, I'd be the troubled picturesque,
Francis Bacon impasto in bloody summer shift,
torn hills a rolling, Act 3 backdrop. This move
would be against nature, survival even.
Yet I want to bring the tree to earth,
fulfil the mandate of my species.

When I walk past this no-name gum,
I dress in careful greens and browns;
the only way you'd know I wasn't a tree
is by sore movement, the bent laurel
leaves of a shaming poetical garb. I aim
to surprise but am never gum enough –
too neat, too coiffed, a garden shrub
with a pencil, not an axe. I'm ignorant of
Eucalyptii nomenclature, sidle past
leafy provocations. A neighbour gives
a disturbed smile. To her I'm a soldier
from a retro TV skit, leaves glued
to a helmet of hair. I hope she understands.
A street empty of trees, of nesting creatures
causing guilt or sorrow, is my simple ideal.

I won't make eye contact with a stupid tree;
the enemy know all about peace and shade.
Survivor guilt. Eyes on the field! Let slip a word,

green or brown – you become nature's target.
Atten hut! Trees teach the slouch-hatted soldier
the deceptions of camouflage, provoke anew
the wild, bloody signatures of white foresters.
I blame trees for straining poetic excess:
'verdancy', 'mote', 'middle distance', 'landscape'.
Like me, the politician plays a useful role,
busily extracting, taking nature down,
teaching poetry a lesson, discipline.

I write to him for permission to shoot.

Warm regards

Your regards melt polymer screens
but you yearn for cooler rapprochements,
for looking or regarding that is neither
coolly cynical nor warmly propositional,
intelligent heating of thought and idea. Oh,
where is that warm looking and seeing
that enables you to look the furnace
of new weather in the eye? Send it regards
of the warm, steady sort, not those
that require you bring a lump of coal
to public meetings, where men huddle
by imaginary fires fed by rolled banknotes,
welcoming you with extractive, double-glazed
stares, regarding the lump as a mummified
brain, an ancient, fond returning
to something you cannot signify.*

---

* On Thursday 9 February 2017, then-Treasurer Scott Morrison brought a lump
of coal into the Australian parliament, ribbing Labor opposition about its energy
policies: 'This is coal, don't be afraid.' Grinning National Party leader Barnaby
Joyce juggled the lump before passing it along to colleagues, while Morrison
articulated the benefits of coal to the assembled chamber.

Moon

For CA Conrad

She has no long view. Dirty clouds wipe
her cratered eyes but space junk
forms cataracts, galactic landfill.[*]
The poet lands in darkness, writing
celestials that can't accelerate.
Debris orbits her *vitreous humour;*
poems fall slow. Gravity is serious.

Men dream the short view: colonies, moon
landings, quick fortunes – predations of space,
water and body. Moon-fooled sailors
thought it navigable; Selene's pocked skin
sheds doubt. In steel caverns, industrial
moonlight produces jet-fuelled scrap.
Shine a light. Don't blame earth's
one fixed satellite for Eden, junked.
Silver-suited and telescopically enhanced,
men travelled 240,000 miles to the moon
and realised the long view home was perfect,
delicate, like nothing ever seen.

---

[*] Space junk has been amassing since the first human-made satellite, Sputnik 1, escaped Earth's gravitational pull on 4 October 1957. NASA chronically underestimates the amount of polluting space junk, focusing on junk moving at speeds that places space shuttles and satellites at risk. An estimated 500,000 pieces between 0.4 inches and 4 inches across join larger fragments of debris that sit within 1250 miles of Earth's surface in 'low Earth orbit' where satellites, such as NASA's Earth Observing System fleet and the International Space Station, reside. Even minuscule debris fragments pose risk for spacecraft, due to their incredible speeds. Adapted from Maya Wei Has, *National Geographic,* 25 April 2019.

Save as

After John Donne, 'The Sunne Rising'

Busy old sunne turns muscly thug,
your cheesy, factor-fifty smile's
no apocalypse circuit-breaker,
a poor man's contraception
in a populous *worlde*.
'All here in one bed lay' you say,
behind fire-suited hands, love's
season a national disaster,
poetry's ash-in-glove.

Your solution, dear, is pack
the hybrid wagon with the rags
of modern time and drive
to the other side, as if time
apart in remnant bush will cure
when leaf and love are done.
Thou art teary now; who can blame?
Islanded with your cold keyboard,
you wouldst not stare down
cruel importunate sunne,
reverend beams blinking sour
and say: 'I promise even so'.

Thine age asks dis-ease; don't confuse
flight and politics with sunny hope;
since Monday, seasons fail to rhyme,
climate-denying princes play us,
while you elegise the fight.
Each time you hit 'save as',
world fails to attach to *worlde*.

Winds come, uncalendared, ropable.
Taxonomy, seedbank, soul, heart –
all quaint alike *no season know nor clime*.

Meanwhile, weather drones rise
from *state to stratosphere* like offerings,
though there never was a god
of meteorology or air, only phrases
all honours mimic. That is the double
sphere of loneliness. Our prayers
and tappings – ekphrastic, ecstatic,
don't conserve. The brute sunne
is twice as happy as 'we'. Its day job:
To warm the world, that's done in warming us.

Australian coal man

Fastens a jet necklace round the clean
neck of his clean wife. Her bronchial problem
and lignite stare never clear up, even in summer,
terrace doors shut against the fiery pall.

He deliver undeliverables. A fool from marketing
tells him coal is 'col' in olde English. Musing,
he thinks that sounds like a mate who'll
meet him halfway on any mad scheme.

But etymological shifts are coked conceit,
the agency ditty betrays. He's raped
and immolated 'Col' until he sighs
like a showgirl breathing 40% emissions.

But his days are clean and just; he tweets
all-ordinary joy over dirty coffee and fossil-
shaped pastries. Thermal and metallurgic
are up – no sunset industries.

But the lungs of the future hang outside
the corporate body like runners over suburban
powerlines. At night, chimneyed dreams
stack against him; his pale children accuse.

One day he wakes to stillness, house
a white-shuttered cage, the stuttering
city, dark as a pit, world canary quiet,
shoes swinging in the breeze.

Coal and meter

The poet digs down a decade
with her plastic pen, rests by
the ancient seam, earth's
little black dress boudoir-veined.
Poet and coal are looking for love,
unelectric *coup de foudre*.

But things proceed awkwardly.
The poet moves to the unburned bed,
can't resist old conveniences:
metaphor, simile, desk of wood —
mocking pit lights that insist
on metered form and usage.

What's left: tired enjambments
of surface talk, absence of mood,
the customer IDs of ghosts, a shared
cigarette after extraction.

Casuarina

(*Allocasuarina verticillata*, Gadabanud Country)

You and I were not introduced
though we depended on whorl and root.
From the start, you asserted wind-shifting
ambiguity, not foolish breezes of poets.

In sharper light your leafy foliage
was thin-branched deception,
offering no handholds, only
petty shade, spindly cladodes.

Up close, we saw you were not lonely,
craved no understorey, life teeming
beneath. A canopy of others, jostling
ladder trees, repulsed you as ancient

harbingers of 'personal space', though
this was our modern right. We grew
angry with your hushed demands,
muscling in with axe and saw, though

you'd long claimed clearance around
the grove of yourselves. We planted
out your filtered allopathic shade until
your terrifying windy rapture ceased,

love's stern susurrus, married element
and oak, whispering 'impostor'.

The poem after forests

1.

Take the Wikipedia entries for 'forest' and 'water'
and change the tense: forests *are* to forests *were*;
water *is* to water *was*. Relieve yourself of the pressure
of time; the poem forgets/forgot ruminants, rockfaces
and oceans. Never mind that Bo Peep admonishes
/admonished us, all ribbons and bows, a pointed foot,
farthingale aslant. Her pretty rhyme never has/had
a fund for forests. Native creatures. Streams.
Sequestered pulp and coal, not words, now
light/lit and warm/ed whole worlds.
Don't pay twice for nature poems, petticoated
energy 'undeliverables' that see/saw no
'additional abatement in emissions'.
Fire, coal, tallow, electricity — burn/burnt by
the quiet desk, so that the poet lamely
shepherds/shepherded toxic run-off. By Friday,
the last millennial pasture is/was all blue ruin.
Bo Peep calls/called out 'Oh no!' half-heartedly, pinkie
extended. This art, she notes/noted over tea, is/was part of
a great accounting. Yet banking days are/were
numbered; company reports drive/drove home weak
couplets, all couch/ed mumble-geddon,
while the board don/ned cloaks and crooks.
They strike/struck Bo-peep down in remnant
pastures green; accountants with pin-prick eyes reliably
hum/med 'Where Sheep May Safely Graze'
as figures for dead forests and toxified water
come/came in. Corks are/were popped
(the last gnarly specimen long since harvested),
as profit margins are/were toasted all over again.

2.

Meanwhile, water is/was traded, no longer free
or pure, from the source. Plumbing is/was never democratic;
imperial engineering always a class illusion, channelled.
In African equatorial heat, women trade/d sexual favours
for half a litre so their children live/d another day.
Rhymed seas, rivers, oceans fail/ed to assist; do/did not form
munificent reservoirs. Brook, pond, waterfall, stream,
ghost/ed the modern shepherd–poet's banked emissions.
Let's face it, the quiet desk is/was once a tree.

The poem's future dehydrates, plays with time. Tense.
Take the Wikipedia entries for forest and water.
Do not drink these or wander in the leafy shade
of comparative cultural definition. Your last task,
changing time: forests *are* to forests *were*.
Water *is* to water *was*. Relieve yourself
by the imaginary tree. There is nothing to drink.
Lie down with your plumbed conceits.

Drought faith

After the fountain in St Peter's Square, Vatican City, by Carlo Maderno, 1612

Paintings turn water into wine but can't change
it back. Ignore the shocked reproach of fountains;
drunk on myths of perpetuity, tyrannical assurances,
ancient watermarks − coursing blind.

When Vatican City turn off one hundred fountains,
the host sloughs on the tongue like an airline cracker,
the guy who did water and wine − lost in his cups.
But the good pope prevails, hands opening
in drought-supplicant grabs. Cameras drink it up as
blackbirds drop dead in Wednesday's pie-bake heat.

Pilgrims mass, wildfire whispers down the line:
He's left us for his summer house. Some fall to their knees,
black cloth streaming on cobble. They were famous
for it, the princes of the church, pure liquid doctrine.
Now it's too hot or too late to shout big words:
'transubstantiation', 'climate change encyclical'.

Yesterday, plastic bottles were as numerous as the faithful,
both blessed from the source. Source? What is craved ...
River gods self-harm as the privatised aquifer hoards;
nasone drip down rank littered streets. Meanwhile,
cardinal thirsts find their own spring; at St Peters,
small boys rap by Maderno's dry font.

Death in Venice

We knew better than to come back,
marry ourselves underwater –
no better church, our dull bones said,
than history's murk lagoon.

In sleep, marble lions roam
with intent. Eyes closed,
stone paws gentle our necks,
force ersatz land claims.
We resile, ash-scattered.

There! Our old selves crawl
back to meet us. Marble, flesh
and water compact but remnant
amphibians won't photograph.

Balusters mimic dessicated spines
from anatomy primers, but bridges
sigh beneath floodlines.
Death proffers a courtly hand, but
the glove in the canal's polyester.

In weedy tabards we catalogue
history's last move, time's wet
archive. Ghosts croon low, beg
a cup of silt on poured streets.

This courtesan glides between fixities,
hoarding art, indescribable jewels.
On Thursdays, she wears a dirty mask
and mothy velvet; cats climb higher.

New gliders come. At San Marco,
Nigerian hawkers constellate night
with flying gizmos, soft light falling
on carpets of broken Murano.

Ocean liners, bigger than destinations,
spew particulates, glide on. Half-gilled,
we rise, open-mouthed, to the surface,
hoping to see ourselves there.

A short history of aluminium cans

I learnt at can school that
the drive to buy inheres
in object death and all death,
the aquifer on the dry plain
drained by corporate straw.
For my part in that, I'm sorry.
See, for small farms, the broken
stream's a spit river; life
won't carbonate there.

What's left is aftermath,
demise of brand auras, refund
potential, crushability. Test
my mettle; watch alum shear,
red and silver letters crumpling.
Remnant syrup, post-guzzle,
flocks my tin skin, ghosting
well-bled tributaries.

Once upon a time I was pulled
from a caf fridge, retro logo
concealing sweet fraud.
Patent desire sang city streets
in ring-pulled polyphonies. *Enjoy!*
Now annual reports exchange
falling hits of carbonated sugar
until a cola-dipped quill signs
my death certificate
in careful brown stokes.

The weary coroner, zealous
for detail, downs me as he types,
signs off on the fizz of life.

Glad: A life

After Justin Hofman's photograph, 'Sewerage surfer', 2018

They rolled me, rolled me happy, stickifier added to polyethylene. Proto-gladness was sprayed on airforce fighter planes as protective sealant. Those planes were wreathed in smiles! That was kids' stuff compared to my work in food preservation. In my time, I covered a gazillion *hors d'oeuvres,* sandwiches and sweetmeats, ensuring crispness, flavour, extended life. My role was assured, though the name 'Glad' was yet to come. As the *juve* 'Wrap', I brokered smooth running of late-capitalist mastication rituals, my contribution coming close second to that of alcoholic unguents (though that's surely for an overdue anthropological study to find). In the early days, during my long years at Atomic,™ I was a flexible friend, supporting millions of happy, sighing ladies as they stretched me over a trillion snack, dinner and dessert plates. They too seemed accepting of their roles. Plasticated hair, twinsets. Demure social presences.

By 1960, Atomic™ had a media spokesman, 'The Man from Glad'. Alas, he was no conversationalist. When pressed, he knew nothing of the chemical history of plastics. Oh, if I only had time, dear reader … His *doppel*-injunction was this: 'Why take chances, get GLAD!' and 'Don't get mad! Get GLAD!'. We weren't close, but as his mantras unrolled over the unsigned planet, my reach became gratifyingly global. Some people wanted my autograph. Or his. Truly. I was an investor's dream. No condom or plastic glove knew such starry success. Condom and I still don't speak. Jealousy, I guess. But sometimes, a little lonely with it, I go hand-in-glove. No advertiser exploited the canny potential of the word 'love' hiding in plain sight in the word 'glove'. Glove, for her part, was saddened by that particular failure of imagination. Was not 'glad'. But humility made her easy to be with. We talk often, related by direct polyethyl and polymer lines.

Late career, I was promoted from half-eaten roast chickens and day-old sandwiches to wrapping suitcases of first-class fliers. This was a stretch. Then economy class argued for hygienic suitcase protection. The assumption that case locks were potentially faulty, case shells weak, especially the posh ones, was dubious. But, *Glad* to the rescue! I donned my cape. Wrapping machines were installed in airports. They couldn't produce me fast enough. I became confused as to what was case, what was carcass. Fatigued, I messed up. I was sent to a Nestlé sanatorium in Switzerland to rest and recover. Then, with chemical tweaking, a little therapy, I came back stronger than ever. No mere retro coverall, *moi!* I speak modestly of my achievements, but I've won awards. Been lionised in literature.

In the novel *Infinite Jest* by David Foster Wallace (1996), the final year of commercially subsidised time is referred to as the 'Year of Glad' in reference to the imaginative brilliance of my second parent, Union Carbide. Though we came together late, in that year of truly terrible assassinations (in '63, cellophanes and crepe paper were brutally retired and worse awaited Tupperware), it was UC who named me, who brought joy to kitchens worldwide, commercial and domestic. Gladness was shared when my aunt and uncle, Proctor and Gamble™, invited me in. I was on the cusp of retirement, yet market-steady. I rose to a late challenge. I would not be retro. My heart fills to think that by then there was so much of me in the world. When naysayers began to collect and recycle me, I was only briefly troubled.

These days I'm forgetful. I spend my time rolling off benches, out of bins. I make my way down passageways and out into streets. I hit bin bag, floor, road and updraft with the assurance of a beat poet. When I find a stray drain, I am off on holiday! Aloha! Escape to the sea.

If this seems a false gesture of spirited independence, remember it was you who provided the infrastructure for me to cover, conserve and protect. My holiday luggage, tightly wrapped, glistens brightly. I sing songs of gladness as I set out, the smell of sea salt in polyurethane nostrils. I've posted photos of my successes. In this mammoth task I have assistance from others. Every day (though semi-retired) I make myself over as a marine Lorelei. I cover everything in my wake. I strangle and caress, caress and strangle. Oh Lord, I am GLAD, GLAD, GLAD™.

Pink lake 1, Westgate Bridge

And this is why I sojourn here
Alone and palely loitering,
Though the sedge is withered from the lake,
And no birds sing.

John Keats, 'La Belle Dame Sans Merci'

Under the bridge, candied algae,
algorhythmic, heat the salt lake
into a sunset cocktail. I turn up
with miniature umbrella and straw.
Keats said scenery is boring,
but seldom strolled the toxic lake,
blaming daemons, not dye vats,
for withered English sedge.
Underwear models, not faeries,
arrive for lakeside shoots,
pose on reclaimed land like
sequinned wildlife, pink on pink.
Flyover white noise persists,
baffling bird calls, reproductive croaks.
Afterwards, the models pack
into vans. Behind smoked glass,
pink palms press against silver duco
letters that spell *S-E-X-Y-L-A-N-D*.
From afar, they spell 'Sedge Lake'.

This is why I soujourn here.

Pink lake 2, Westgate Bridge

One man is out there, under
the grey-shadowed span,
fishing the high-salt spume
for hot pink yabbies
for his hot pink wife
and hot pink children.
He can't wait for a hot pink
statue of Captain Cook
to staple lead sludge.
At school, he mistook Cook
for a colonial masterchef,
slaving out of a hot naval
kitchen all the pink day
and all the pink night, salting
the pink land he cooked
for king and country.

Book club for dry towns

We were inlanders. Men of hoar-frosted
country halls with baked, craquelured
weatherboards who felt there was nothing grand
left to imagine. Most of us had never seen
the sea's great roiling quilt, ghost-netted
turtles strapped in with every semblance
of mother love. Hemingway and Hornblower
were natural choices, though piratical tomes
were never as fine as *Master and Commander.*
After talk, book club moved swiftly to the pub.
In the main drag, late on a moon-limned
Tuesday, town notices read as civic poetry.

Inside the bar, the mounted, taxidermied
cod with rheumy eyes knew a single-use
destiny, as if he too were a bookclubber
in search of a river on a page. Flow.
His shrunken, scaly chest and mournful
stare told of old troubles: thiefdoms
of water, friends transmogrified into
seafood baskets. All the mighty river corpses,
the barmaid heard, had been interred
in soft plastic and dumped on the edge
of town. A great silver stink rose.
It's a fuckin' scandal, the bleary
bar-stool vet cried. We drank off books,
as Maurie wept. On the way home,
as we argued the toss on everything,
a bag floated over moonlit landfill,
looking, like us, for love or use, a drain
to the sea, suffocations of meaning.

Nightjar

We have no protection, are thirsty as gin.
Cloudy stanzas form strange weathers
of the mind, careless proleptic elegies.
Our jar is mostly empty as a bird falls
from the sky. Vacant-eyed, possums
assemble by beach umbrellas and eskies.

At the servo, cars rev as the cat peels
the rental verandah back. The bird's mate
flies off to nested Shangri-La and
heat's opiate dulls the cat's claw.

How to help stunned bird past taxidermied
midnight, endangerment, twitching certainties
of mourning? Mottled plumage mimics
the broken branch, the beak, twig-like.
No trick evolved for predator mercury.

Put the nightjar in a washing basket,
says the soft-voiced animal welfare officer.
Cover him with light blanket or towel.
A man will come for him and the possums.
Watch for cats, they're the big danger.

We pull towels over our heads,
beat sundown and wait with the bird,
for the man who surely knows of jars half full,
of cool-blooded hope, patient shifts
of scale into feather under glass.

Horn

Unbandaged rhinos in the cheap seats
know that the removal of their cousin's
horn for aphrodisiac purposes won't better
stockpiles of love poetry, alter the
performance of the Iowa hardware man
mounting his third wife, Gloria.

After the latest poaching, a glossy nature
reporter was called in, stumbling
over the word *Rhinocerotidae,*
omitting the class words *mammalia.*
Meanwhile, the savannah bled.

Make-up did over the corpse's eyes, rhino
as Rudolf Valentino, taxidermied exotic.
The New York zoo relations wept hard at that.
Among the crash, Eliot was known for
grumpiness and flashes of sunny
kindness. True, he was overweight,
but still thought handsome by some.
That didn't mean he had to die, his niece sobbed,
cramming into the home theatre provided
for less fractious zoo creatures.

They turned down the sound, reporter miming
to sparse trees, grasses bent under jeep wheels,
bloodied bulk of Eliot slumped behind her like
a morning sacrifice, and she, the glossy priest.
Through blurred tears his cousins, far away,
imagined the delicate, respectful thrumming

of kind bush ants coming quickly, with
reasons of their own, to triage the wound
and take what was theirs by nature.
They would not use the word 'poach'.

I want/don't want a place

I want a place
past poisoned soils where
moony cattle stare and low,
asking patient why.
But abattoirs dissemble, cool
metallic grins hidden behind
slaughtered hills, shower-
capped workers falling out
at 4pm, blanked by blood,
grim mesentery tangles,
a record day's offal weight.

I want no zoos, no brittle
arcadias, rewilded bridges
spanning eight-lane freeways,
birthmarked by old roadkill.
Close underfunded ecology
centres, cheerful Alice pushing
forms and crying *Sign, Give, Leave us
a message. Please! Please!*

I want no old-growth flyover,
concealed battery shadow:
hens, coal, uranium, light, heat —
time leaking and degrading,
guarded sites that mine and mine
and still say 'mine', all mine.

Let the aggrieved 'I' cede
to hummed insect edicts,

silent fish councils, weary
roars of trash-loving bears,
the understorey's riotous
demand for fire. Retire 'I';
let it hang its head
and not conspire with
mea culpa's last egotism:
lazy planetary leave-taking.

De-bunk moss-dreamed no-place,
caretaking outsourced, poorly paid.
Let thronged 'us' walk shadow places
that tell tales of toxic time and make time
full again, ask more than patient why.

Acknowledgements

'My father's thesaurus' won the 2020 International Peter Porter Poetry Prize and was published in *Australian Book Review*, January–February, no. 418, 2020, p. 53; 'Ring-in' was published in *Australian Poetry Journal* (eds Jill Jones and Bella Li), p. 67; 'The art: Ultramarine', was shortlisted in Empathy: 2018 ACU Prize for Poetry and published in the associated prize anthology, pp. 32–33. 'The poem after forests' was published in *Rabbit Journal*, no. 29: Lineages, pp. 98–100, 2019, and commended in the Venie Holmgren Environmental Poetry Prize.

The Rimbaud quotation is from the poem 'Democracy' in *Illuminations: A Season in Hell and Illuminations*, trans. Bertrand Mathieu, BOA Editions Limited, Rochester, New York, 1991, p. 81.

The quotation from Evelyn Reilly is from 'Broken water', *how2*, vol. 3, no. 2, 2008, www.asu.edu/pipercwcenter/how2journal/vol_3_no_2/ecopoetics/reilly.html

The Alison Whittaker quotation is from the poem 'A love like Dorothea's' from the collection, *Blakwork*, Magabala Books, Broome, Western Australia, 2018, p. 5.

Val Plumwood's words are from her article, 'Shadow places and the politics of dwelling', *Australian Humanities Review* no. 44, pp. 139–150, 2008.

My gratitude to Puncher & Wattmann, especially to editor David Musgrave. Thanks to Miranda Douglas for designing the cover so beautifully, to Morgan Arnett for layout, and to Bella Li and Lisa Gorton for their generous words and for time spent. I am indebted to editors and publishers Peter Rose, Jill Jones, Bella Li, Jacinta Le Plastrier and Chris Wallace-Crabbe for publishing the poems listed in the first paragraph above. Thanks also to Melbourne University Arts Faculty, which supported this book with a publications subsidy. Italian-themed poems included in this collection were written as a result of an Australia Council residency at the B. R. Whiting Studio in 2017, and I thank the Council for that life- and work-changing opportunity.

This book would not exist without input from trusted readers, Brendan Ryan, Anthony Lynch, Suzy Freeman-Greene and others. Especial thanks to Anthony Lynch for love and support, and to my dog, Leonard Woolf, who forced me to walk and re-work the bones.